I0464396

Best Selling Products

How to Find Them, Sell Them & Grow Your Business!

By
Kimberly Peters

For

The Entrepreneur Skills Institute

Disclaimer

This publication is designed and intended as an informational publication only and not a definitive action plan for any specific product, business or business situation. Since every situation is different and every person is different, it is not possible for one approach or technique to deliver optimum results every time. So it is up to the reader to determine which parts of this book, if any, apply to his or her own business or situation. The writers, sellers and distributors of this publication assume no responsibility for the use or application of any or all parts of this book.

Contents

Introduction

If it were only so easy as to just create any kind of product and be assured of a multi-million dollar payday then life as we know it would be so much easier. But unfortunately, product creation, or finding an already created product which has yet to really "take off" is far from a slam dunk. If you don't believe that, ask any successful business owner or entrepreneur and they will quickly tell you. Although they are successful, they have also had a few "clunkers" in their day.

The point is that if you want to be successful you are going to have to take a few risks when it comes to deciding what to create or what to sell. But the key to success is not avoiding these risks but instead to make those risks as small as possible. And that is exactly the purpose of this book.

Over the years I have designed many products, some of which I thought were 100% sure-fire winners. Then I discovered, much to my dismay that they were just not going to sell. After a few of these, mixed in with other products that were successful, I decided that, in order to be as successful as possible, that it made sense to create a kind of blueprint so to speak of what an ideal product should consist of.

Then, I could use this blueprint and compare a new product idea to it to see just how well the product measured up. To my delight, I found that this helped me abandon products that were losers and to concentrate my efforts on those products that had the best overall chances of succeeding.

Was this foolproof? Hell, no! But it was extremely helpful in allowing me to be more productive and cut down on my losses. Most of the time when I looked back and closely examined a failure I found a few things that I had not thought of that helped me refine my approach. To my surprise as well, a couple of borderline products actually did very well and exceeded my expectations.

I also found this blueprint especially useful in finding products that already existed but for some reason had either not done well or had not been marketed effectively. In those cases I was able to take a poorly known products and bring it to the marketplace and make some money on it.

For those of you who do not develop products and instead sell other people's products such as affiliate marketing, this will work for you as well. It's all about picking the right product to sell so that you make the most money.

There are two keys to using this book to help identify or create new products:

First, be honest when you go through the blueprint and compare your product against it. Sometimes we become so emotionally invested that we tend to overstate the positives and drastically understate the negatives. But when we do that the only one we are fooling or cheating is ourselves. Why waste time and resources on something that is just not going to sell? Be open and honest and if something doesn't look like it will work, find something else that will and move on.

Second, give each part of the blueprint an honest effort. Don't think something isn't important because it very well might be. Spending an hour or two at this stage can save you tens of hours in the future promoting something that just isn't going to sell. Or, we might waste time promoting something in the wrong way because we do not totally understand the appeal of the product.

Which brings us to one last important part of using this blueprint.

When you go through the blueprint and analyze a product in all the ways we are going to talk about, you will come out of the experience understanding the product at a level you never thought you could understand it. You will understand its appeal, who is likely to really want this product (your target audience or market) and several other things that will help you sell and market your new product more accurately and properly.

All this boils down to choosing the right products and marketing these right products in the right manner so you sell many more of them than you normally would. Because having a great product often isn't enough. It is knowing what to do with that product once you have it. By using this blueprint, you will automatically find the best products and know how to market them effectively as well.

So, let's get started!

Part One:

The Psychology of

Buying

Why People Buy What
They Buy & Why They
Choose Some Products
over Others

Customers are People Too

In order for us to identify or design the perfect product, we need to be able to put ourselves in the mind of the customer or the people who we want to purchase our products. This is important because it is not us we have to satisfy when it comes to designing a product but instead the people who are going to buy it.

That is something that many business owners and marketers don't fully seem to grasp. It makes no difference how we feel about any given product because we are not the ones who are going to buy it. We can love something to death but if customers don't buy it then it is not going to be a commercial success.

Fortunately it is easy to place yourself in the position of a customer.

That is because customers are people just like you and I and we pretty much like and want the same things in life. While no two people are exactly the same, and while some people will like or value some things more than others, we will all pretty much have similar core values and needs.

For example, everyone like to get a great value when it comes to anything they buy. Virtually no one wakes up and says "Today I'd like to be taken advantage of today and buy a piece of crap that I don't need and I'd like to pay a premium price for it." Though that sometimes happens to all of us no one goes out of their way to experience it. Instead, we all run the other way whenever possible to avoid it.

Many of the factors we are going to discuss when it comes to products are known as "subjective" factors which means that the importance of these factors and how they are interpreted rest mostly with the customer. This means that since what is important to one person might be totally unimportant to another, that there is no one perfect or correct answer. So a lot of these decisions are going to be based on feelings or opinions.

In order to get the most accurate answer to how customers are likely to feel, we have to take off our seller's hat and put on our customer hat. We have to look at things from a customer point of view and not as a seller. Very often this will cause us to have a completely different point of view.

For example, as a seller you might look at a high margin or selling price as being a very positive thing because you make a lot more money on high margin products. So the more you can charge the more money you make. As a seller, you like this. But as a customer, you look at high margin or high-priced products as a negative because it costs you more to purchase these products. Because of the high cost you might decide to purchase a cheaper product instead.

The same thing could be said for features as well. You could love a product you created because it had a long list of features and would do just about anything. But customers might find the product too feature rich and difficult to operate and want something simpler. These customers would greatly prefer ease of operation and simplicity than an extra set of rarely used extra features.

Both of these examples are perfect examples of why it is what the customer wants and how the customer feels is so much more important than how the seller or product creator feels. Customers buy products not the developers or sellers.

As you go through the blueprint that is going to be outlined for you over the rest of this book, think about the features and factors pertaining to the product from the customer's point of view and not your own. This can be easy once you get our mind used to looking at things differently.

Design your product with the customer in mind. Ask yourself what the customer would like to see and design your product, or choose your product, according to what the largest majority of customers are looking for. If you like something larger and heavier but most people like the product lighter and smaller, then make it lighter and smaller so your sales will be larger and you will make more money.

The best designers and the best marketers are able to set personal feelings, opinions and ego's aside and act mostly on customer demands and preferences. Even though we think we might know what's best, what we know isn't always the most important thing. We often have to ask ourselves the question "Do we want to be right or do we want to sell more products and make more money?"

Most of the time you will gain insight into the product and will be able to reduce expenses while producing a much more in-demand product. But sometimes you will have to change the product to incorporate more of what the customers want and this might cost you more money. But despite the extra costs, we need to produce the product the customer wants.

In the next chapter we will deal in why is so important. In fact, this is more important today than it was just 10 years ago and it will continue to get more important in the future.

Options

Here is another part of the consumer buying process that is critical for any marketer and business owner to understand. The more options available to the customer, the more demanding and critical the customer will become. And since the options for just about anything have drastically increased since the advent of the internet, we need to be especially responsive to the demands and needs of our customers.

In the early days of the Old West you bought food and supplies from the one General Store in town. You used the one Blacksmith and stayed in the one Hotel. You drank at the one bar and ate at the one restaurant. In other words, you consumed or purchased what was available and you had better like it because there were no alternatives.

If you didn't like the beer they served at the bar, it was too bad because you couldn't get any other beer anywhere else. If you didn't like the food at the restaurant, that was too bad. You either ate it or you cooked your food yourself. When someone has no choices, they have to put up with what they can get.

Now fast forward to today. Every town has dozens of restaurants so if you don't like the food at one you can go to another. If you don't like the food at one store, you can buy it at another. And there are more kinds of beer available now than one could ever have imagined. So you just go to where your favorite is on tap or sold. Those businesses who do not have what the customers like will find themselves out of business because customers now have choices and can go where they get the most of what they need or want.

But since the internet became so popular customers have an almost unlimited selection of products and services all within a few mouse clicks. Which means they can almost instantly compare product against product and selection against selection. And they can do this all without leaving their home or driving to a single store.

Plus, customers are no longer limited by what is in their town or local area. Through their computer they can purchase products from anywhere with just a few clicks of their mouse.

So they do not have 5 different choices like they used to they now have 500 choices. And believe me when I tell you that many customers will research every one of those choices before they decide on what they are going to purchase.

What all of this means to the seller or product developer is that they have to design or provide products that best suit the needs of their customers or those customers will buy elsewhere. It might not be good enough to hit 5 out of 10 features to close a sale. You might have to hit all ten for some people in some products. This is because they have so many options available to them.

There are some people who feel that their product is "good enough". But their version of good enough might not match the customer's version. Plus, "good enough" will limit your market share to only those customers who are not all that demanding or whose needs are not that comprehensive. If you want to create a product that appeals to the masses, it is going to have to be very, very good because it will be prepared against the competition.

Another thing to consider is that if your product is "good enough" to compare against other products but is not better than the other products, there is little incentive for a customer to go back to your product to make the purchase. Once they have exhausted their search to find something better and they determine that the product they looked at last is just as good, they will buy that one and not yours. So your product should be better, not just equal, or your sales will not be very good.

When deciding on a product to market or produce, remember that customers will but the product that best suits their needs. They will only buy something that comes close when there is not a product available that is better. No one likes to settle when they don't have to. And when there are so many other options available to the customer, they are not so willing to settle when they don't have to.

Product Resonance

Product resonance is a term for how well a product appeals to a customer. It is how the customer reacts when they see, hear or read about the product. The stronger the customer reacts to the product the greater the chances are that they will purchase it. Because of this, we want to design or find a product that has a large "Wow! Factor" to it.

Product resonance has several factors that go into it. How a product looks and feels, how it is marketed and what it means to a specific customer all translate into whether or not that customer will purchase that product. In many ways, every item of the product blueprint has some connection to product resonance.

You probably have experienced product resonance many times in your life as well. Think about when you last went looking for a new car or a new sound system or some other product and one product just stood out from the rest for some reason.

You might not even have understood what it was that made it stand out but it did anyway. What you experienced was product resonance.

The best products resonate with the widest audience. They provide that special something to more people than any other similar product. It makes no difference how it accomplishes this, all that matter is that it does.

Sometimes product resonance comes from a certain situation that exists in the customer's life at the moment. If you product is perfect to address that situation, and the problem is serious or strong enough, that could translate into an easy sale. It's like selling bottled water in the desert. Any water will look like heaven in a bottle to a thirsty man!

So what does this have to do with picking or developing the perfect product? Well, we need to pick products that are going to resonate with the most people. Then we are going to have to design advertising and marketing program to make sure that we present that product in the right way.

It is not enough for a great product to have all the features the customer needs. It is not enough for a product to solve all the customer's problems and be perfect for the customer.

While both those factors are important, they are also meaningless if the customer is not aware of them. So we need to pick the best product and make sure the customer is aware of all that it does and why it is the perfect product for them.

We cannot expect the customer to connect the dots and discover that the product is perfect for them. We have to take them by the hand and hit them over the head with all the advantages and benefits this product has to offer. Only then will the product have a chance of resonating with the customer.

We need to paint a picture of the product in the mind of the customer and that picture has to be bright and vivid and extremely positive. It has to connect with that customer in such a way that they feel the product is special and a perfect solution to a need or needs. All of this has to be accomplished without the customer necessarily understanding it is happening.

Just like that new car just somehow appeals to you or that sound system just feels like the perfect one, so should any product you design or choose to sell resonate with the customer.

Buying is a very emotional process and product resonance is a very strong emotion factor when it comes to deciding which product to buy and who to buy it from.

Does this resonate with you?

I hope so.......

Features & Benefits

One common mistake a lot of people make is trying to sell features of the product to the customer. Or deigning products based on features rather than benefits. Features are great but unless a customer understands what the features really do and how they will benefit from having a product with those features, the customer likely is not going to be overly impressed.

Put in other words, customers do not buy features they buy benefits. For example, an extra capacity washer doesn't mean much to a customer but a washer that can wash twice as many clothes in the same amount of time probably does. The benefit to washing more clothes at one time means you can do more laundry in the same amount of time or the same amount of laundry in less time.

In that example, high capacity was the feature and saving time, energy and convenience were the benefits. Benefits are important to point out because unless the customer understand just how the product is supposed to make life easier or better for them, they are not likely to buy it.

The product designer or creator needs to understand the value of including a certain feature into the product as well. Features cost money and time to make part of a product. So unless the particular feature has a benefit or value to the end user, it is not worthwhile to the product or add to its overall success.

So when you are developing a product or analyzing an existing product, do not look for features. Instead take a feature and decide what the benefits are to having that feature. This is where a LOT of product designers and marketers go wrong. They design a great product with great features but they don't take the time to make sure the customer understands the benefits of those features.

Like most anything else in life, if a person is not aware of a particular benefit in something it is like that benefit never existed. So create a product that has features and benefits and make sure that your customers understand both. Because anything less is just not enough.

Consumer

Confidence

Part of the buying process includes the amount of confidence in the mind of the customer. This confidence is important on several different levels of the buying experience. If it is missing or lacking in intensity this can result in a lost sale or at least in postponement of the purchase of the product.

There are several different type of confidence required to complete the average sale. The more expensive or larger the purchase the larger a role confidence will play in the purchase decision. This means confidence is a lot more important in the purchasing of an automobile than it is a loaf of bread or a gallon of milk.

Here are the different types of confidence required to complete the average purchase:

Confidence in the Suitability of the Product

In order for a customer to even consider purchasing the product they have to feel a certain level of confidence that the product will do what they need it to do. The higher level of confidence they have the more likely it is that they will eventually purchase the product. If they have a very high degree of confidence in the product they might purchase the product right then and there which is what you want to see happen.

Factors that add consumer confidence in a suitability include features specific to the problem that needs resolving, the products appearance (color, size, weight, design and other items) as well as the sales process and overall marketing campaign. The more you can tie the product directly to the specific problem or need the more likely you are to close a sale.

Confidence in the Overall Quality of the Product

People want things to last. If every customer had their wish, all products would last indefinitely and always remain in style. But that is not reality and most customers understand this. But they still want a product that they are confident is going to last a long time and function properly during that time.

For customers who already own a similar product they might have comparisons that influence how they feel about the product. For example, if they had a product that lasted 20 years they might expect the new one to last that long as well even if that expectation is reasonable.

Factors that influence quality and longevity might be weight, overall design, product feel, length of warranty, brand name recognition and reputation as well as customer opinions and comparisons with other similar products. Customers often will but the product that they feel has the highest quality and therefore is more likely to last the longest period of time.

Confidence in the Person or Company Selling the Product.

Many customers are skeptical when it comes to sales people, marketing materials and product claims. They feel this way because there are so many scammers and outright lies out there in advertising today. Claims such as "Lose 20 pounds in one week without diet and exercise" naturally make people more than a little wary when it comes to what they read or are told regarding products.

Because of this brand recognition and reputation will play a huge role in getting people to believe claims and purchase the products. For an established business, their reputation might be enough to get people to purchase. The same can be said for a products reputation once it is established in the marketplace. But this can take a lot of time to establish and even then, not everyone will be aware of your reputation.

The best way to convince people to purchase is by being honest and upfront during every part of the sales or marketing process. Advertise and market your products to be good and make sure people understand what they can do but do not be deceptive and try to convince people that a product is something more than it really is.

During product design or selection, find or design products that do what they say and possibly even a bit more. Being known for selling or marketing only the best products will help you a great deal later on. Do NOT sell or design a cheap product to make a quick buck as this will destroy your brand and make it almost impossible to sell anything else to a customer later on under the same brand or business name.

All of these confidence factors are very important in not only convincing a customer to purchase your product instead of another but also directly influence whether the customer purchases now or later.

Since they are in your store or website now, and might not come back later, you want to do everything in your power to get them to purchase now.

Because of this always take consumer confidence into consideration as you choose or design products and when creating your advertising and marketing campaign. Because anything you can do to increase consumer confidence will help you r business not only close more sales today but also close more sales in the future as well.

Perceived Values

The last thing we want to discuss when it comes to why people buy certain products is perceptions. Understanding the importance of perceptions is important because they require a different line of thinking than we are accustomed to.

First of all, we need to understand that perceptions are what the customer THINKS is correct when it comes to something. It makes little difference whether that perception is right or wrong because the customer believes it is correct. So as far as the customer is concerned, it is the truth. So we not only have to deal with the truth and reality, we also have to deal with perceptions.

For example, if we have a great product that does exactly what it is marketed and expected to do and it does it extremely well but the customer perceives it to be a total piece of junk, as far as the customer is concerned it is junk and there is no way they will ever purchase it.

So it is not just the case of being right or wrong, it is the case of whether or not we can complete a sale.

So how exactly are perceptions created? What happens to make customers perceive something in a certain way?

Basically we form perceptions based on life experiences. Every time we witness something, hear something or see something, we form a perception. The same thing happens when we read something as well. Anything and everything we experienced in our lifetime helps us form a perception.

Perceptions help protect us and help us make the right decisions in certain circumstances. Perceptions help guide us through things we should avoid or things we should be afraid of as well. Our perceptions are our reality and we base our thoughts and reactions on those same perceptions.

As far as products are concerned, our perceptions are based on product reviews, advertising, comments we have heard, practical experience we have from actually using the product and several other things. If the information we get is accurate, we will develop accurate perceptions.

But if the information or experience is flawed or otherwise inaccurate, we will develop an inaccurate opinion and perception.

For example, if we fail to follow instructions and have problems with the product, we might tell other people the product is crap and they might form a false impression that the product is poorly designed. The fact that the product is great but the user was defective makes no difference. For most people, their perception is their reality.

So as we choose our products, or develop them, we must make them as easy to use and have instructions and owner's manuals that are extremely easy to understand. This will help us minimize problems and negative experiences which can result in a poor perception of both the product and your business. This is important because a single bad experience might take up to 10 good experiences before a positive perception is created.

We are telling you all of this because it is not good enough to have great products. It is also not good enough to be right in any given situation. Neither of those is nearly as important as having the customer or consumers perceive that you have good products and that you support those products effectively.

Establishing a strong brand image is all about perception. Your products might be just as good as your competition but if your brand image is better then you will close more sales. Previously we talked about the importance of consumer confidence and it is that same consumer confidence that allows a positive perception to be established with the customer.

So please understand that perceptions are extremely important whether they are true or false. Even a totally wrong perception can do damage to you and your brand if it goes unaddressed. So whether or not something is true, try and resolve the error or make sure the issue is dealt with effectively.

If your product or service is perceived poorly, find out why and take steps to correct that perception. If you have problems, or if there is something that your customers do not like, it is up to you to correct it and correct it quickly. After all, if your customer perceives that something is not right with you or your product, they can always go somewhere else.

And believe me, they will.......

Part Two: The Characteristics of Success

What Helps Make a
Product Good, Great or a
Total Flop!

Mass Appeal

A successful product is a product that is used or need by the largest possible audience. That means that the product is needed by almost everyone for one reason or another. Naturally the more people that need what you sell the more people you have that can become potential customers.

For example, let's say you manufacture special pants for men who are over 7 feet tall. Now there is a market for those pants because people over 7 feet tall are usually going to have longer legs than you and I so they cannot simply go to the store and buy their pants off the rack. So there is a market there.

But there are many, many more men who are 5 and 6 feet tall who also need pants and that particular market might be thousands of times larger.

So it stands to reason that if you made really nice pants in those sizes you would sell a lot more than you would if you just sold to the 7 foot men. The trade-off is that you probably would have more competition as well.

The point we are trying to make is that for a product to be successful it needs to have a large market to sustain it. This is also true when it comes to products that have a lot of competition. The market must be able to sustain the product or you should not invest in that particular product.

If there is not a sufficient market then even if the price is perfect and the quality is excellent there will just not be enough people who need the product to justify selling it. So when evaluating a product get a handle on how popular or large the potential market is going to be before making your decision.

Market share is important in the design of product as well as sometimes we can add features to make it desirable to a wider or larger audience. So when you are choosing a product or designing your own, always look for ways to make it appealing to more people. This will give you a larger group of potential customers which will translate into more sales and more profits.

Keep in mind as well that markets change over time.

What might be a large market today might disappear tomorrow as technology changes over time. Technology has a way of making the popular items of today totally obsolete tomorrow. More on that later.

Examples of Products That Have Mass Appeal

Food, clothing, telephones and accessories, books, personal grooming products, vitamins, healthcare products.

Long or Short-Term

The best products are the ones who are strong and unique enough to withstand the test of time. While there is definitely money to be made selling one-shot, short duration products, the big money is made selling and producing products that are likely to be around for years or decades.

Every product has certain expenses that are part of producing the product but are unrelated to the actual cost of making the product. Costs like research and development, market analysis and testing are all part of choosing or producing a new product. These expenses are then spread out over the life of the product.

So if you can continue selling a product for 10-120 years, all of those development and testing costs can be spread out over that long period of time. But if we can sell a product for just one year or less, then all those costs have to be paid off almost at the start.

This can make it more expensive to sell short term products.

For example, if it costs us $10,000 to develop a new product that we will be able to sell 10,000 units of over the next year, the cost will work out to be approx. $1.00 per unit. If the selling price of the product is low, that $1.00 can represent a significant cost for that product.

But if we can sell that product for 10 years and over that time sell 100,000 units the cost would work out to be 10 cents instead of the one dollar. This might not sound like much but with product development and testing for some products costing a lot more than our $10,000 estimate, being able to sell something for a longer period of time just makes sense.

Another reason for having products that continue to sell for a long time is that they provide continuity for our business. Almost all products will have some kind of lifespan and the longer that lifespan is the longer we will be able to count on those products for income and sales. This will enable us to gradually phase our older products and bring in new ones so there will be a gradual change in our product offerings.

Always have an appropriate mixture of both long and short-term products in your business so you can not only take advantage of the latest trends with short-term products but also have the stability and profits of long-term products to keep sales coming in when the short-term product sales begin to lag. Keeping both types of product in your business will help you maximize profits while also improving stability.

Long-term products are also great because we already have them listed on our website or catalogs, entered into our computer systems and we also have their marketing and advertising materials designed as well. Though there will be slight modifications over time, the cost and inconvenience of having to prepare these materials from scratch can be avoided when we sell products for longer periods of time.

Another benefit of long-term products is that they can develop a following over time as more and more people purchase them and tell their family members and friends about them. Since word of mouth advertising is both free and very powerful, we want to leverage this as much as possible for our business. If people recommend a product to someone and you no longer carry it for some reason that does not look good for your business. Though the customer might find another similar product when they come in, there is also a chance that they will become frustrated at not being able to get what they wanted from you in the first place.

Examples of long-term products would be, common tools like hammers and screwdrivers, food staples such as milk, butter and eggs, and clothing like shirts and pants etc. These are the products that change relatively little over the years and are likely to continue to sell for the foreseeable future as well.

Examples of Long-Term Products

Bread, milk, clothing, shoes, gasoline, automotive products, tools, books

Examples of Short-Term Products

Fad items, limited run items, certain forms of technology (because technology makes some product obsolete every other year)

Seasonal or Year-Round?

Seasonal products are those products that mostly sell during a specific time of the year. During that particular time of the year's sales might be very high only to taper off once that time of year has passed. There are definitely products that can create an entire year's worth of sales within just a few months so do not automatically discount a seasonal product from your inventory.

Of, course, if you had to choose between a product that sold well for just 3 months as opposed to products that sold well for all 12 months, we all would agree that the year round products are better additions to our business. After all, these products will generate income for you all year long.

But depending on your industry and your location, you might not have the luxury of having a year round product to add to your business. For example, if you sell holiday decorations, those products are only going to sell during the months preceding the holiday itself.

After all, no one buys Christmas decorations in May unless they happen to be on a great sale!

Seasonal products can work well if you are able to take advantage of two things.

First, if you are able to find appropriate products for each time of the year then you will always have a product producing income for your business. For example, if you sell holiday decorations and have products for Christmas, Easter, July 4th and Thanksgiving, there would be products becoming popular with customers all year long. Though some will perform better and sell more than others, you would still be making some kind of sales all year long.

Second, if you are producing your own product and can have it ready in time to take full advantage of its sales cycle then it might pay off for you. Even then, you need to be careful when stocking inventory because the demand for some products drops like a rock after the season is over.

All things being equal, year round products will give you more sales and better overall performance. Your sales will have fewer spikes and you will be able to forecast sales and profits more accurately. But that does not mean there is no role for seasonal product.

There are businesses who make a years' worth of profits in just one season. In fact, some businesses just open for one season, do a ton of business and then close until the next year. If that is something that interests you, all you have to do is find the right seasonal products, develop a following and just work a few months out of the year. Or, open a couple of seasonal business keeping each one open just during that particular season!

Just like in the last chapter where we talked about balancing long-term and short-term products to take advantage of all opportunities, so should we balance our product offerings to include both seasonal and year round products? Ideally our business should do relatively well on just the year round products and get a well-deserved boost in products from the seasonal offerings.

But with enough seasonal products, spread out over the entire year, a business that develops a good following can do very well with seasonal products as its primary source of revenue. It is a balancing act but it can be done.

One important consideration when it comes to seasonal products is your ability to accurately forecast inventory needs and anticipated sales of these products. You want to be able to stock enough product to fulfill all your sales needs but not so much that you are left with a lot of excess inventory after the season ends.

Excess inventory is like money sitting in your warehouse and some products do not sell well the next year when new models and versions come out.

Examples of Year-Round Products

Food, clothing, automotive products, tools, healthcare products, vitamins

Examples of Seasonal Products

Christmas decorations, Christmas trees, holiday decorations and items, gardening products (in some areas), plants, hunting and fishing products.

Solve a Problem

Behind every successful product there is a problem that needs to be solved or a need that has to be addressed. That is the reason the customer is even thinking about possibly purchasing the product in the first place. If the product does not address a need or solve a problem for the customer, it is not likely that they will buy it!

This is the most basic driving force behind every sale. People buy stuff not because they really want to but because the product will somehow make their lives easier, better, more fulfilling or more prosperous. But behind each of those things is a need.

We buy information books because we have a need to learn something.

We buy food because we need to eat or because we are hungry.

We buy a car so we can go different places.

We buy dandruff shampoo because we want to get rid of our dandruff.

So we should ask ourselves "What problems or needs does our product address, resolve or fulfill?" Don't look at features but instead the problems those features are designed to address. That is what is going to drive sales. All the features in the world will not help you sell a product unless the customer understands which problems or needs will be taken care of.

Because of this many products are what we call "reverse engineered". By that we mean the designer or inventor will take a list of problems that need to be solved and then design a product to accomplish all of that and more. The more problems the product addresses, the more popular the product will be.

It also helps to have the product address major problems. These are the products that are really in demand. The more serious the problem the more likely the customer will be to purchase something to eliminate or at least reduce that particular problem.

For example, if you developed a product that cured bad breath, people would buy it as long as it was not all that expensive because bad breath for most people is an inconvenience and not a major or traumatic problem for them. So that product might sell well if the price was low enough that people thought it was a worthwhile product to have.

But if you developed a product that cured cancer, diabetes or any other major disease, not only would it sell extremely well but people would pay almost any amount for it because it solved a very important and major problem in their lives. If you had such a product, you could name your own price and still sell a ton of it.

Evaluating products based on solving a problem is going to involved a few different criteria. Though not a complete list, here are some of the criteria for how well a product will sell based on the problems it solves:

How Common a Problem

The more common the problem is the larger your pool of customers is likely to be. That means more people will purchase your product if they want to deal with their problem. Though you are not likely to get everyone to buy your product, a share of a larger market is still better than a share of a smaller market.

How Many Problems Doe it Solve or Help With?

If a product deals with or solves multiple problems, this increases the potential market for that product. This means more potential customers and larger sales.

Because of this a product that deals with several problems at the same time will usually be more valuable and sell better than a product that solves one problem.

How Serious is the Problem?

The more serious the problem the more willing people are going to be to purchase your product. Though it might sound crass, the more serious the problem the more desperate the customer is going to be to find a solution. If your product does what you claim it does, and it does solve a very serious problem, you just might have people lining up at your door to buy it from you. And they are more likely to pay a premium price for it as well.

How Many People Have This Problem

We already talked about a problem being "common" but that is also a very relative term. A problem can be common to older people but not to younger people. It might be common to overweight people but not to normal weight people. Or, it might be more common to people in one part of the country.

So even though it addresses a so-called "common" problem, we must define common. Naturally you want your product to address as common a problem as you can possibly find. Everyone eventually will get the "common cold" so if you have a product that will help with the common cold, there will be a whole lot of people who might buy it because it effects young and old, male and female and people in every part of the world. It just doesn't get more "common" than that!

What is the Cost vs. Perceived Value?

As we said, the problem must be important or serious enough to make people want to take action and purchase a product that deals with that problem. If the problem is not considered that serious, people might just decide to live with it or deal with it themselves first.

Because of this your customer must feel that the benefits provided by the product are more valuable than the price of the product. If you charge $9.95 for your product it had better be perceived to provide more than $9.95 worth or perceived relief or most people will not buy it. People with bad breath might not consider this important enough to spend money on something that cures it. But when someone is given a diagnosis of cancer or other major disease, they will pay you anything for your product if it will cure their disease and save their life.

So the ideal product should solve multiple problems that effect the largest number of people and it should do it at a price point that people feel is very attractive for the problem it solves. This is important because even though people have problems they need fixed, they are always looking for a cost effective solution at the same time. Only when people become desperate do they not care about price.

Examples of Products That Solve a Problem

Just about every product solves a problem or addresses a need or it wouldn't have been developed in the first place! So it is not so much whether or not the product solves a problem but instead which problem and how well it solves it.

Fill a Need

Having a need for something is a little bit different than having a problem because a need is often a personal desire. When we "need" a new dress or to lose weight, it is not because our health is at risk or because we don't have anything to wear to dinner on Saturday night. It is because we need these things for certain reasons not because they represent problems in our lives.

We go out to eat because we feel the need for food because we are hungry. So to satisfy that need we go to a restaurant and have a meal. Or we pick up food to cook at home. In any case, we have a need to eat because we feel hungry. The only time this becomes a problem is when there is no food to be had. Then the need after a while becomes a problem.

Much the same way as problems, the stronger the need, the more likely people are to purchase a product and the more they are likely to pay for it.

For example, you might not want to pay $1 for a bottle of water on the street but if you were in the dessert and thirsty that same bottle of water would be worth paying $5 for! It is the law of supply and demand.

The same parameters that we discussed for problems also apply to needs. The more people that have the need the larger your market is going to be and you will have more customers and hopefully more sales.

The more urgent the need the more likely people will purchase your product and also be more willing to pay whatever price you want for your product. If the need isn't urgent, the price people are willing to pay goes way down. They are also much more likely to postpone their purchase or just think longer about whether they should buy now or later.

So when it comes to your products, determine which needs they address and determine just how significant or large these needs usually are. This will help you not only choose the right products but also come up with the right price point as well. When both of these things come together the result is that you will sell more product and you will sell it for more money.

Examples of Products that Fill a Need

Much like with solving problems, every product fulfills some need or it would not have been created in the first place! So look at the product and determine what the need is that it addresses. If you can't find one, then you obviously do not need that product!

Make Life Easier

Here is something else that products should be able to do for the customer. Everyone likes life in general to be easy yet there are many things in life that are just plain difficult or time consuming. If you have a product that can make a difficult task easier or just make anything easier to accomplish, you might have a winner on your hands.

"Easy" is a key marketing focal point for many products. In many cases the product works just as well as other problems performing the same function but they accomplish that in a much easier fashion. Entire companies and industries revolve around this simple yet very powerful concept.

For example, you see shelves full of detergents and additives that help get our clothes cleaner in less time. We have floor products that enable us to clean and polish our floors in minutes.

And then there are general household cleaning products that promise excellent results with just about no effort.

No one likes to spend their energy doing something they don't like to do. If they can off-load those tasks to someone else or purchase a product that will enable them to complete the same task with much less effort, they are likely to purchase it.

Think about something as easy and simple as sweeping the floor in your home. It is not difficult and it doesn't take a ton of energy or time yet people are paying hundreds of dollars for a machine that will do it all automatically! Think about that for a moment. Several HUNDRED dollars just so someone can place a machine on the floor and press a button so they don't have to sweep!

People purchase self-propelled lawnmowers, at a premium price, so that mowing the lawn takes less effort as well. In fact, power tools to accomplish all kinds of lawn maintenance and gardening have pretty much replaced the manual tools our grandfathers had used. All of these new power tools exist because they made difficult tasks easier.

People just like "easy". They will pay for "easy". If you can design a product that makes something that is now difficult easier, that might be a big seller. It's a simple yet very effective marketing method.

So find a problem that a lot of people don't particularly enjoy and either find or develop a product that makes that task easier. Make the product easy to use and easy to get great results. People do not always like easier if the results are poor. In order to have a successful product them you have to have something that makes it easy to get great results. When the customer is finished using your product they should be pleased with the results.

You might also have a top selling product if you improve an existing product to make it even easier to use or enable it to get even better results. The arrival of top performing cordless battery tools are a perfect example of taking an existing product and making it easier to use.

All of that happened because someone realized it was a royal pain in the butt to string extension cords all over the place to use their drill or hedge trimmers. Add to that the thousands (probably millions???) of people who have cut, chopped, run over or otherwise destroyed extension cord after extension and an idea was born.

Turn conventional power tools into cordless, battery operated tools. The first generation of these tools did not work all that well.

They were weaker and the batteries didn't last very long. But now we have tools that are equal to or even outperform corded models and the batteries are smaller, lighter and last longer. Again, all of this came from a problem and an idea to solve it.

As with a lot of other factors, if you can make something easier at a price point that people feel is worth it, they will buy your product from you. But even that automatic floor sweeper, though it does make keeping your floors cleaner with less effort, would not sell very well if it cost the customer $5,000. At that price they will just sweep the floors themselves.

So keep in mind the type of problem, how difficult or inconvenient it is and what the value of making it easier really is. The determine the correct price point and if you can sell the product at that price and still make a decent profit, you might have a winner on your hands.

Examples of Products that Make Life Easier

Tools (especially power tools), eye glasses, hearing aids, canes, air conditioners, heaters,   telephones.

Make Something Faster

This is the second part of the "fast and easy" marketing approach. Not only do people like things to be easy, they want them done fast as well. If you can take something that takes a long period of time to complete and speed up that process significantly then customers just might start flocking to your doors to purchase your product.

"Fast and Easy" are two things that go hand in hand. We already talked about easy but the second part, fast, is equally important and sometimes even more important. After all, time is one thing you can never get more of in life and any time we can get something done faster and have more time left over for other things that can be a powerful motivator to purchase.

Think about all the products you have seen that concentrate on getting something done faster. Microwave ovens cook food in the fraction of the time an oven could and there are hundreds of microwave products to make cooking anything easier and faster. Ask anyone who has made popcorn the old fashioned way and had to clean up all that oily materials after they were done how much they enjoy zapping a bag of microwave popcorn!

We all live in a very "entitled" or "instant gratification" type of world right now and it is likely to just get worse. People want what they want and they want it now. Not in an hour or the next day but they want it now. So they search out the products and services that will give them what they need in the shortest period of time. People are just not willing to wait for anything anymore.

So much like the "easier factor" either find or develop a product that takes a common task or process and makes it faster. The time reduction should be significant and it should also be easy to use while getting the same or hopefully better results than you would have had without the product.

The greater the time savings the more valuable the product will be in the eyes of the customer. After all, no one is going to pay you for a product that takes 5 minutes off a 3 hour project!

In that particular case I would think your product should take at least an hour off the process. Half the time would be a lot better and a lot easier to market.

When it comes to marketing any product, time savings and making things easier are prime marketing approaches and tools. If you can hit these on the head with legitimate and impressive claims, you just might have a winner on your hands.

Examples of Products That Make Things Faster

Tools, cleaners, appliances, calculators, electronics, certain services, machines

Make Someone More Desirable

This is an area where entire industries have been built and turned into multi-billion dollar profit centers. Any product, or line of products, that help make people more desirable in the eyes of others has the potential to make the owner millions! Unfortunately, it is also an area that is chocked full of scams and inflated claims so there will usually be at least some skepticism by the consumers that will have to be overcome.

For as long as anyone can remember, both men and women want to look and feel better and younger. They also want to become more desirable to the opposite sex and to each other depending on the situation. Marketing and advertising over the decades has convinced people that aging gracefully or not having the perfect body is a curse that no one should have to live with. And of course, they have the products that can solve all your problems.

If you have a product that can help people lose weight quickly and easily and will actually deliver that result in a healthy manner, people will buy that product from you. But that product will also have a ton of competition from hundreds of other manufacturers and stores with the same claims. So while the product may be great and help solve a real problem, marketing it effectively and actually getting people to notice it are two different things.

Cosmetics are a multi-billion dollar industry and their sole purpose is to make people, both men and women, look better, younger and more attractive. People flock to these products hoping to look 10 or 15 years younger just by rubbing or brushing a product on their skin. They do this for various reasons but all you need to know at this point is that these products sell.

As we said there are a ton of scam products out there with claims such as using this product will have women falling all over you and that using this exercise plan will give you rock hard abs in just 4 seconds a day for one week. These ads will also show pictures of people with perfect bodies or nerdy looking guys with supermodels draped all over them.

If your product helps someone become more desirable in the eyes of others, then you might be onto something. But you should also keep in mind that we are not just talking about personal or physical appearance. This is not just about attracting others or the sexual attractiveness aspect of life. We are referring to anything that makes anyone more desirable for any reason.

For example you might have created a book that shows people how to create the perfect resume that will help make them appear more desirable for a job. In this case your product will help someone appear better to a prospective employer and help them get that all important first interview.

Or maybe you have a product that shows people how to become more comfortable in social settings when it comes to conversational skills. In this case you would help people appear more confident and at ease when talking to people they might not know very well. This would make them more desirable in social settings.

There are very few limitations on what you can do to help someone look better in the eyes of others. You can concentrate on personal appearance, interpersonal skills, employment skills and a host of other ways you can make someone look better to other people. If the need is strong enough and common enough, your product could be very successful.

When marketing a product that is designed to make the person look better, younger or just be more desirable to someone else, be careful to market it honestly and keep your claims accurate and realistic. Always remember that you have a brand and image to protect and that false claims can ruin your brand overnight.

You also should be aware that there are rules and regulations about what you can and cannot say in your ads. There are also regulations on what you need to do in order to substantiate and back-up those claims. Since there could be heavy fines and other penalties for making false or exaggerated claims, it is always better to be honest and accurate when you make any claims about what your products can or can't do.

Examples of Products that Might Make a Person More Desirable:

Make-up and cosmetics, weight loss products, self-improvement products, educational products, personal grooming products and services, etc.

Make Someone Feel Better

Products that can make someone feel better, either emotionally or physically have great sales potential. These are products that help improve the overall quality of life by making people happier and live with less stress.

Though there is a difference between making someone feel better physically and making someone feel better about themselves emotionally, both often have the same effect. So products that make people feel better are usually very much in demand. Especially if they deal with a common problem that people can address on their own without medical intervention.

For example, producing a product that helps people lose weight effectively and in a healthy manner might accomplish both goals.

The physical loss of weight might make the person feel better physically because they do not have to carry that extra weight around all day. But the weight loss might make the person feel better emotionally as well when they see themselves in the mirror and see that they look slimmer. They would also feel better when they try on clothes and see that they are too big after the weight loss.

Some products also help people do things that give them a great sense of accomplishment and this can also be a component of making them feel better as well. Learning a new skill, for example, might give someone the confidence they need to allow them to feel better about themselves at the same time. This component is something that might be found in certain products that you never thought of as making people feel better.

So any product that makes a person feel better physically or emotionally can have a significant value to that person. The more people with that particular issue or problem the more valuable that product could become.

When designing a product or looking for an existing product that you will sell, look for ways that this product might make someone feel better.

From the obvious things like reducing or eliminating pain or making someone feel better physically, do not forget the emotional aspect or the confidence the product might help instill in the person using it.

If there are benefits of the product that will help the person feel better emotionally or physically, make sure to address them in your marketing and advertising because these can be powerful incentives to purchase the product.

Examples of Products that Might Make You Feel Better:

Healthcare products, massage products and services, healthcare services, physical fitness / weight loss products, etc.

Make Someone Healthier

When it comes to purchasing products, there are few things more powerful than having a product that helps people live healthier, and possibly longer lives. Any product that will allow people to live longer and healthier, as long as the claims are accurate and legitimate, will sell. Entire industries revolve around these particular products.

Weight loss products, for example, are part of a billion dollar industry. Why? Because they hit so many of the "buying triggers" of the customer.

They help you lose weight which is widely accepted to lower blood pressure, the risk of diseases like coronary artery disease and diabetes as well as other health-related issues.

They help improve quality of life as it is easier to move around when you weigh less and the stress on your knees and other joints is far less as well. Improving someone's overall quality of life is something that can make a product fly off the shelves if it really works.

The list of these types of products is a long one. From vitamins and supplements to weight loss products and exercise programs anything that helps make someone healthier will do well on the market as long as it works as described and produces the benefits it claims.

When you consider that a person's life is the single most important thing to them, and that they usually are strongly motivated to live as long as they can and in the best health that they can, then any product that helps them achieve these goals will usually be well received. After all, there is nothing that motivates people more than staying alive and feeling good.

When it comes to health if you can combine a product that makes you healthier with something that is easy and fast, that will usually hit a lot of the "must buy now" buttons a lot of people have. This is especially true when someone has a health issues that they can do something about but are having a hard time doing so. If you can show them an easier and more effective way that gets results fast, you will have a lot of new customers!

Examples of Products that Make People Healthier:

Vitamins, health-related products and services, weight loss programs and products, health education, medical issue education and assistance and other health related products and services.

Save Someone Money

If you have a product that will enable someone to save some money by using it, then you are bound to get some interest in it. People are always willing to get more information on anything that will enable them to save money or make money. If your product will save people a LOT of money, then you can usually sell it for a premium price as well.

Perhaps the most common products today that we often hear about when it comes to saving money are solar panels and energy efficient lightbulbs. Companies are popping up all over the place selling solar panels and other services and they all use the same sales pitch. Every one of them concentrates on the amount of money the customer will save on their energy bill.

That is the prime motivation for buying these products.

While they might tell you how good the product is for the environment and how you will lose less energy which translates into the utilities burning less fuel and creating a better and cleaner environment that is all just window dressing.

People but these products because they want to pay 30-50% less on their electric bill. They purchase energy efficient light bulbs for the same reason. While I am not saying these people do not care about the environment very much, I will go out on a limb here and say that very few people will shell out $20,000 so the air will be a tiny bit cleaner. They paid the 20 grand because over the years this system will save them 50 grand.

As I said, that is the motivation and that is what closes the sale!

If I am paying someone $50 to mow my lawn every week, then I might think it is worthwhile to spend $1,500 on a riding mower. In about one year I will have saved enough to pay for the mower and from that point on everything is pure profit or savings!

For the same reason I might spend $500 on a snow blower so I won't have to pay the neighborhood kid $50 every time is snows! Plus, I won't have to break my back if the wife thinks I should shovel and not pay someone anyway!

But suppose I am paying someone $100 a month to provide a product or service for me that I cannot do myself for some reason. If I knew of a product that would allow me to do these things myself and save that $100 every month, I would be interested.

There is a direct relationship between money and time. For those of us with more time than money, we will be more receptive to doing something ourselves provided that it is not too difficult, time consuming or requires special education or skills. For these people, their time can save them money if we give them that option.

For example, if you create a product that teaches someone how to change their own oil in their care, that will save them money. Or if you create a manual on how to winterize your home pool or sprinkler system and save that $150 charge at the end of summer, people will be interested.

The most profitable and easiest to sell products are those products that enable people to do things that need to be done several times a year. We bought that lawn mower because we paid to have the lawn cut every week. If we only had to cut the lawn once we would never have purchased the mower.

The best thing to do is find things that need to be done every year, or every month or hopefully every week then create a product that will either teach someone how to do that task or, even better, do it for them. This allows them to save those yearly fees they have to pay people to do things for them.

A perfect example is a personal favorite.

20 years ago I installed a sprinkler system in my yard. Since I live in a cold climate every year you have to blow all the water out of the line so it doesn't freeze and rupture the line. That costs roughly $100 a year for about 10 minutes work.

But for roughly $5 I made a fitting that I used to connect my home air compressor to the sprinkler system and I did the blow-out myself. It took about 20 minutes and every year I save that $100 (probably costs a lot more now) by doing it myself. Even if I didn't have the compressor I can buy one for $150 one-time expense. Over the 20 years I have saved well over $2,000.

Now, if I created a product that made this process easy enough for every homeowner to do themselves, do you think it would sell?

Yeah, it would.

Another form of saving money are products that make it less expensive to accomplish or do something. Energy efficient washing machines, for example, wash more laundry and use less water and electricity than standard models. So every year you would save money on utilities by using these machines.

Over the years there have been a ton of products that save people money by enabling them to do things like do their own haircuts, repair their own appliances, save money on utilities and by doing a host of other things without paying for it. The more money a person can save by purchasing your product the more likely they will be to buy it from you.

Make Someone Smarter

There is an entire industry built around products that help make people smarter or more qualified or just tech them a new skill or ability. These products are very popular with a significant percentage of the population. If you have a product that teaches someone how to do something, depending on the subject matter it could be quite popular.

Information products such as video's and / or books have a huge following for many people. With services and labor costing more and more these days many more people are turning to do-it yourself publications and product to learn how to do something themselves. This can result in a huge savings for the consumer and make these products quite attractive.

Information products such as e-books and paperbacks, or even PDF documents have the distinction of being very easy to deliver and produce as well. Once the material is organized and written into book format, they can be delivered digitally for little to know cost. Therefore profits are much higher and prices can be made lower thus making the product more desirable and profitable.

How-to or other educational products are usually also easy to create as well. If you have a particular skill or talent yourself and are able to put it into pictures and words, you have your information product right there. If you do not already possess the knowledge required then you can research it or even pay someone else to share their expertise with you. With an almost limitless number of subjects you can create several info-based products and sell them on your website.

The subject matter should be appropriate for the do-it yourself person. For example, if you wrote a book about how to grow a healthy garden that would likely sell very well if advertised in the correct places. This is because there are a lot of people who have or are thinking about starting a home garden at their home. Every gardener would be a potential customer for your info-product.

But if you are a brain surgeon I would not advise you to create a do-it yourself brain surgery book.

That is not a skill that can be easily taught to someone without the necessary background or skill sets. Plus, the number of people looking to do their own brain surgery at home would be very limited. But I must say you might sell a few copies as gag gifts! You never know!

Today even video's and CD's are easy to reproduce and there are some online services that will create a paperback book or CD for you and mail it out to your customers for you. The cost is reasonable and you do not have to get involved in the packaging or delivery process either. In fact, you can create a website, list your info-products on it and then do nothing except count your sales and transfer the money to your bank accounts!

In order to have a successful info-product it should be on a widely known and interesting subject and it should teach a much needed or popular skill. Just like any other products the larger the number of people seeking this particular knowledge the more copies you are likely to sell.

Info-products are a great thing for the new business owner to sell because they are inexpensive to produce and can be delivered digitally to save money. There is no inventory and as we will discuss later, they can be delivered instantly which is something that a lot of your customers are going to find compelling.

Examples of info-products are:

How-to books, training videos and DVD's, books, manuals, PDF documents and other publications. Training kits and other training materials would also fall under this category.

Easy to Purchase

Make no mistake about it, customer like things easy. They want products to be able to be found easily and they want to be able to purchase those products as easily as possible. The more difficult we make something for the customer the more likely they are to leave and look elsewhere.

Making something easy to purchase usually means giving people as many options as possible when it comes time to purchase. People should be given different payment options such as multiple credit cards, PayPal for online orders as well as accepting checks and cash at times as well.

If you are selling via a website the product should be easily located on the internet and easy to find and identify once people are on your website.

Descriptions should be written clearly and adequately describe the product and what it is designed for. Pictures, size, weight and other pertinent information should be given as well.

The payment process should be streamlined as well. If people have purchased from your before it is a huge advantage to have their information stored somewhere so they will not have to enter it every time they wish to order something from you. Amazon has a one click button that allows you to order some products with just one click. You click the button and pre-saved information populates everything from address to credit card information. It just doesn't get any easier than that.

Products that are easy to purchase are the ones with the fewest items and choices. This also helps with stock as you only have to stock one or two models and not 15 colors and 4 different styles. When it comes to ordering easy, simplicity is best.

This is a reflection on your business more than the product but keep in mind that if for some reason you have any product that is difficult to purchase that this might be viewed as a negative by the customer. So choose products that you can make easy to purchase and get into the hands of the customer as easily as possible.

Examples of products that are easy to purchase:

Anything that comes in one or two colors and in just one size. The more options and sizes and colors the more items the customer is going to have to choose from and this can get tiresome.

Easy to Transport or Ship

Though you might not think about it at the time, the ability to easily and inexpensively ship a product to the customer is extremely important when it comes to making a profit on every sale. This is because shipping and packaging can destroy even the most ambitious margins if given half a chance.

The best products are the ones that cost the least to ship. If it costs you nothing to ship a digital product that costs you nothing to product and deliver then you made a profit of the full $4.99. But if you sold a product for $9.99 that was heavy and bulky and cost you $9.00 to ship to the customer, then you only made a profit of 99 cents!

The best products are the ones that can be placed in the customers hands for the least amount of money.

The less you spend on shipping the more profit you will make on every sale. Now if the product is picked up at your store then size or weight might not make any difference. But if any part of your business requires shipping or delivery, then size and weight will definitely matter.

In addition, the shape of the product will make a difference as well. Oddly shaped products might require special packaging and special shipping which can significantly add to shipping costs. So special care should be made when designing or choosing a product to see how its size and weight will influence costs.

For example, if you owned a retail store and someone came in to buy an anvil from you that is OK as they will just wheel it out to the car and drive away with it. But any company trying to sell anvils online or via mail order will incur a hefty shipping charge on every one. If the item is large or bulky enough shipping costs might just price it out of the online business.

Also keep in mind that unless the shipping company picks up from your business or warehouse that you will also have to transport the items to your shipping company as well.

So the larger your average item the fewer you will be able to load into each truck. You will therefore have to make more trips or get larger trucks. Each will cost you and your business money.

Now some of you out there might feel that this is not a big deal because you charge extra for shipping. But the fact remains that the more shipping costs the more expensive it is going to cost you to get it to the customer. Even when the customer has to pay for shipping most customers will just add that cost to the price of the item when deciding whether or not to purchase it. If the shipping costs are too high, the customer will not purchase and you will have lost a sale.

If you are designing your own product keep size and shape as well as weight in mind. You might even want to make a mock-up to see what shipping will cost before committing to producing the products at all. Because shipping does really matter.

Another factor when it comes to shipping is how fragile the product is and how much extra or special packaging is going to be required to get the product to the customer in excellent condition. Because you are going to have to replace any product that arrives damaged, it is important to package things right to begin with.

So a book would be something easy to purchase because it is not fragile or easily damaged. But a glass figurine or sculpture is much more fragile and will require special packaging and special handling in order to avoid breakage. Always keep in mind that there is no profit in replacing damaged merchandise and there is usually a loss.

So, choose products that are light and compact and easy to package. Pick products that are not fragile and are able to be shipped safely with little or no extra packaging. Every added extra or special packaging costs you extra and eats into your profits.

Examples of good products to ship:

Books, pillows, blankets. Sheets, clothing, digital products

Examples of bad products to ship:

Anvils, glass figurines, glass anything, cannonballs, long lengths of pipe or other long items.

Multi-Functional

As every business owner or product creator should be aware of, the more people who like or have interest in a product, the more it is likely to sell. So it stands to reason that the more people a product appeals to, or is targeted to, will result in more sales.

So far we have talked about problems and needs that all customers have and that because we are all different, our needs and problems will be different as well. So it is not reasonable or possible to design one product that will solve everyone's problems or fulfill everyone's needs. So we need to do the next best thing.

We need to find or develop a product that is multi-functional and addresses more than one singular need.

Think about that for a moment. If we find or produce a product that is truly multi-functional, and by that I mean does more than one thing or addresses more than one issue or problem, that product will almost always appeal to more people. This is because we are now addressing more than one group of customers. If the product does two things we are now addressing two different groups of people. If it does 3 or 4 things we now address 3 or 4 groups of customers.

Great products almost always address more than one issue or have more than one function. Take a tablet reader or Smartphone for example. Not only are they phones but they are also cameras, calculators, text messengers, game consoles, alarm clocks and lord knows what else they could do with the appropriate "app".

If a smartphone was just a phone it would be popular. But when you combine all the other features and capabilities it becomes such a popular device among so many different types of people it almost flies off the shelves. If all it did was make or receive phone calls, it would not be so popular.

Multi-functional products also sell better because they do more than the competitions products might do.

Adding features and capabilities helps manufacturers grab more market share and therefore close more sales. Market share is important and having more features and abilities than the competition is one way to easily dominate your industry.

Think about some product you have purchased that were multi-functional and that you actually use for more than one purpose or application. Isn't this product more valuable to you and wouldn't it be valuable to more people because it had more than one function?

A cordless drill not only drills holes but drives screws and bolts as well. You can also use it to polish things as well with a buffing wheel. Your home sound system lets you listen to the radio, play CD's, watch movies with surround sound and for the "old school" people out there, even play records!

I own a gardening tool that has multiple attachments that allow me to roto-till, dethatch, edge and slice the lawn for seeding. Because it does so many things it was well worth the $400 price tag! If it only had done one of those things I probably would not have purchased it and certainly would not have paid that price for it!

A multi-functional product will not only appeal to more people but will often justify a higher price point as well.

Having more than one use will make is more desirable and will increase the amount of people who will buy it. Multi-functional capability just makes a product more valuable to more people

On the flip side, making something do too much can also turn off customers. Multi-functional is good but if there are so many different functions that the product is extremely difficult to learn how to operate, that is a negative.

Also, if making something multi-functional also reduces the performance of the product at the same time that can be a problem as well. Most people would prefer a product that does one or two things really well as opposed to a product that does 15 things with not so great results.

Last but certainly not least, multi-functionality often comes at a higher price and if having several functions raises the price to the point where the product is too expensive, that will hurt sales as well. Remember that the product people are considering buying represents a certain value to them. If the price exceeds that value they will not buy it. This is especially true when all the extra features and functions are not needed by that person.

Examples of multi-function products:

Certain tools (i.e. a multi-function tool), appliances, electronic items such as sound systems and cell phones, computers, etc.

Unique

If you are selling a product you will sell more of them if they are special types of products that are different from other products. You will also sell more of them if they are not sold in every store or website throughout the country. Having something special or unique helps you stand out from the crowd while also helping you establish and grow your brand image.

A great product does something better or differently than other products. A great product has a unique advantage or feature not available on similar products available elsewhere. These are the products that make customers stop and really look at the product and notice it is different than everything else on the market.

Products with unique or different characteristics make people stop and take notice.

Those products have something that resonates with the customer and makes them want to learn or know more about that product. They see something different and they become curious. Once you have their attention it is much easier to close the sale.

People like to shop around and buy what they feel is the best deal and you cannot blame them for doing so. But sometimes when people see the same products in the same stores they get frustrated and just buy that product at the last store they see it in. If that is your store or website that is great but chances are it will be somewhere else.

But if your product is different and the customer realizes it is different, they stop to examine it more closely and if there is a feature or something else that they like and have not seen anywhere else, they might buy it right there on the spot. They might even pay a slightly higher price for it as well.

If you are developing your own product, you also want it to be unique and stand out from the rest of the crowd on your shelves or on your website. But you also want something about it to be different so that nobody else can sell it. In other words you want your product to be proprietary in nature to protect you and your business.

When you have a proprietary product and have the necessary protection on that product no one else can copy it or sell it without your permission.

With marketing and retail being such competitive businesses, people are always looking for what is selling well and then jumping on the bandwagon with the same product. When you have a unique product and own the right, people cannot do that.

This is important because if you develop your product you have spent a lot of time and resources creating and manufacturing that product. Those costs hopefully will be recouped over time as you continue to sell more and more of them. But if someone else copies your product and creates a lower priced model, your sales will plummet.

When choosing a product or designing one, ask yourself why or how this particular product is different from the other similar products on the market already. If your product is the same as every other product, you can still sell it if it was profitable to do so but you should not waste a lot of money creating your own model if something else already exists. The only exception to this might be if your product could be manufactured and sold for less than the existing products. Then you could sell based on price point and make more sales.

We want people to see different products so they stop and take notice.

We want to capture their interest and their imagination so they can picture themselves using that product or having it in their home. Buying a product of any kind always has both a practical and emotional component to it and having something different and unique is always better for the customer and the business.

A word of caution though. Just because something is different or unique, it still must accomplish its primary function and it must do it well. Making something different but getting lower quality results or otherwise poor performance is not a good thing. People like different and better not different and worse. So choose your products carefully and always go with unique and better every time.

Easy to Understand
or Use

People like easy and they love simple. So it is no surprise that some of the most popular and best-selling products on the market today are the ones that are easy to use and make getting something done as easy as possible. This is because when you are selling easy and convenience, it also applies to the product itself!

I own several products that can do a myriad of things but the problem is that they are so damned difficult to operate I use them for just a fraction of their functionality. All the other functions appear so convoluted and confusing it just isn't worth my while to try and figure them all out. It's not that I am technology impaired or anything like that. It's just that I have a hard time remembering the 57 steps and which buttons to push to get to that particular function.

The problem we have today is that products can now do so much and so many different things that they have gotten so complex and difficult to use that consumers now shy away from some truly great products. They take one look at the online manual and go straight to the next product on the shelf.

Ideally, every product should have one button that turns it on or off and that's it. Or a how-to book should be written so someone in kindergarten could understand it without having a Master's degree from Harvard. Unfortunately, too many products are built by people who have little or no concept about the people that are going to wind up using those products.

A perfect example was a thermostat that was in a home my son recently bought. I was over the house and for the life of me, I could not figure out how to turn the air conditioner on. I called my son and he walked me through the 7 very non-intuitive steps you had to go through just to turn the AC on! Even after having it explained to me I could make no sense as to why the product was designed that way!

Every product you sell should be easy to use or operate. Operation should be intuitive without the person having to consult the owner's manual every time they want to use the product.

If there is an owner's manual for the product it should be written in a clear and easy to understand manner as well. Not everyone using the product is going to have a PhD. In technology.

If the product is information-based, write it so everyone can understand it. Write it on a third grade level so confusion would be at a minimum and the likelihood of using words people might not understand would be rare. After all, the purpose of an owner's or instruction manual should be on getting the right results, not impressing the reader with our vocabulary. Oh, and by the way, skip the tech jargon and fancy technical terms as well. Customers prefer something written in a language they can understand.

Speaking of language, understand your customer base as well and make sure you have products and documentation that coincides with the language that they speak. Even the best written manual or instruction sheet is not going to be of much use if it is written in a language the customer does not understand!

All of this is important to your business for several reasons. First, people need to be able to use what they purchase.

If they cannot figure something out, or if it is too difficult for them to do so, they are just going to return it for a refund.

Now you have a used product you might not be able to resell, at least at full price, plus you have a dissatisfied and probably frustrated consumer as well. Neither are good for you or your business.

Second, even if they keep the product they are going to have a lot of questions and you are going to be expected to have answers to those questions. Which means having trained people available to answer the questions and paying them for the time they spend doing so. This can be a big drain on resources for many businesses.

So, whenever you evaluate a product, or when you are designing a product yourself, ask yourself how easy is it to use? Give it to other people and see what they think about the ease of use as well. This is important because as we design a product we become intimately aware of just how it is supposed to work so even the most complicated procedures and processes appear easy. But having other people test it will give a more accurate indication of how easy it really is to use.

As we said, the best products, and the products that cause the fewest problems, are the ones that are as simple and easy to operate as possible.

So always keep that in mind when choosing products that you want to sell. And don't take the manufacturer's word for it either! Actually try and product and put it through its paces to see if it really is as easy to operate as they say it is.

That is because some person's version of easy might not match anyone else's!

Priced Right

Like it or not, where a product is priced can have a huge impact on how well or poorly a product sells. Determining the proper price point is a balancing act. You want to sell it at the highest possible price so that you can get the largest profits but not that high that the customers just pass it by because it is too expensive.

The right price point is determined by the value that customers place on your product. As long as your selling price comes in under the price the customer feels the product is worth, it should sell well. But if you want more than what the customer feels the product is worth, you won't sell very many at all.

For example, if a customer wants to buy a product to help him with a certain issue, and he feels that resolving that issue is worth $50 to him, he will gladly pay $39.95 for a product that helps him because that price is less than the value he has in his head.

But if you have a great product that sells for $99.95 he probably won't buy it because his particular need does not justify spending that much money.

Of course this is for non-essential purchases. For necessities, it is what the market will bear and what kind of competition or options the customer might have available to them. In other words, if you have to have something to survive, you have no choice but to pay the going rate even if you don't feel it is worth it.

The perfect example of this could be your local electric utility bill. You might feel it is grossly too high but if you want the little things in life like heat, refrigeration and other conveniences of life, you have to pay it. Unfortunately we have far too many of these types of expenses in our lives.

So unless you have a monopoly on a particular product meaning you are the sole source for that product, you are going to have to take special care is arriving at the right price point when it comes to selling your products.

Usually this price point is determined by checking the competition to see what other comparable products are selling for and then pricing your product at a competitive level. It doesn't have to be cheaper but it needs to be competitive.

For example, if you sell a gold plated widget and everyone else is selling similar gold plated widgets for $29.95, yours had better be either $29.95 or less if you want to make more than a sale or two. If you price your gold plated widget at $59.95 you had better have one heck of a superior gold plated widget or you won't sell any at that price!

Some businesses make a mistake of setting a price based on the profit margins they need to have in order to make a profit. So if the widget costs you $14.95 and you need a 3-1 profit margin, you might think you can sell your widget for $44.95 and that this would be a fair price. After all, you deserve to make a profit and if your costs require a $44.95 selling price then that is what you should charge. Right?

Wrong!

The first thing you need to understand when it comes to pricing is that your customer doesn't give a damn about your costs or your expenses.

All they care about is what the product is going to cost them when they buy it. If someone else has lower expenses and can sell it to them for a lower price, they will buy it from them. It's as simple as that unless you can convince the customer that buying it from you is an overall better deal.

So whenever you are deciding whether or not you should be selling or designing a certain product, think about whether you can sell it at a price that will generate a large enough profit for your business. We will talk more about this in the next section of the book but for now, make sure pricing plays a significant role in your next product decision.

It should also be mentioned that sometimes added services and benefits offered by the business, such as free delivery or in-house service often will allow the business to charge a premium price for what they sell. In many cases price is just one component of the overall value of purchasing the product through a certain business.

Which is exactly why you need to carry the right products and fully develop your brand and your brand recognition and reputation. Because those two things just might allow you to sell the same products at slightly higher prices than your competition and still make a ton of sales doing so.

Crazy, Weird or Odd!

Let me start out by saying that there sometimes is no rhyme or reason or even common sense when it comes to what sells well. Sometimes the craziest, weirdest and just plain stupidest products fly off the shelves because they hit a particular nerve with the buying public. If you don't understand what I am saying, just think of the Pet Rock. If you don't know what that was, Google it. It remains one of the most amazing and confounding retail successes to date.

Crazy or weird products are very popular with an amazingly large percentage of customers these days. There are stores who earn an amazing income just selling stupid stuff you never though would have a prayer of being successful. Yet they sell this stuff by the boatload every month.

But the problem with these types of products is that unless they are already hot sellers and you want to get in on things late in the game, it is difficult to determine which is going to be the next big seller and which is going to be the next total flop. This is because with crazy or weird products common sense just does not work.

Over the years I have seen some really weird and strange stuff and have even bought some of it as gag gifts or just for my own amusement. So there definitely is a market that exists for this kind of product although for the reasons stated above it might be a bit risky when it comes to choosing the products that will sell. But as I said, I have bought some strange things and I am sure others do the same things as well.

I would caution anyone thinking about selling these types of products to avoid purchasing items in very large quantities until the demand has been confirmed. Even then, do not buy a lot of product as the lifespan of some of these products has proven at times to be very short. In other words, what sells today might flop tomorrow.

One last bit of caution. If you are selling one product at a time either online or through advertising then you really are not building a brand so each product choice will have limited effect on the other. But if you are building a brand, which I strongly recommend that you do, try to choose appropriate products for that brand.

Some gag gifts or strange products are less than tasteful and while accepted by many people might also prove offensive and disgusting to others. Only market and sell products that support your brand and represent how you would like your brand to be remembered by your customers. If you are going after the tasteless market, and there is one, that is fine. But if you are not, then be careful which products you choose. A few sales now could jeopardize many sales later.

Attractive Packaging

While they say you can't judge a book by its cover that is exactly what a lot of people do when it comes to choosing their next purchase. They don't particularly read the product description or get into the details of what the product really is and other things. Instead, they look at the packaging and if they like what they see, they buy it.

Most people are visual people and we buy what we like to see. That is why advertisers use sexy models to sell their products and why certain models of cars are designed in particular ways. We often have certain images or characteristics that trigger buying impulses and our packaging should reflect that.

Packaging should look impressive and not cheap unless your business is a low price-based business.

But packaging also imitates and suggests quality as well so having impressive packaging also gives the impression that this is a quality product and not a piece of junk. But since packaging also costs money, we often have limitations on what we can provide in the way of packaging.

Keep in mind that people often see the packaging before they see or touch the product. So all they have to go by is what is on the package and how the product is represented in that packaging. Packaging is also an integral part of the marketing and advertising process as well so the features and benefits as well as other information needs to be on it as well.

If your business is an internet business then packaging might not have a direct influence on what products the customer might buy but when they get the product delivered and they open it, their initial impression of the product is going to start when they see the box. So online or retail location makes no difference. You have to have quality packaging.

Your packaging can follow any design that you desire but keep in mind that packaging has two functions. The first is marketing and advertising which we already discussed and the second is to inspire confidence in the product. In other words, the packaging should make the customer feel that this is the perfect product for them when they see it.

Depending on the type of products you sell color schemes and layout may have a significant influence on how successful your product will be. Some colors sell certain products better than others so it might be worthwhile to have someone design your packaging for you if you have the resources to do so.

Regardless of how your packaging is designed, it should always be honest and ethical and not deceptive in any way. Having pictures showing the product doing unreasonable things or being used in unreasonable ways is sometimes frowned upon and might even subject you to legal action and fines. So package your products in an attractive manner that inspires confidence while remaining accurate and ethical.

Last, but not least, remember that packaging adds both size and weight to your products that therefore will have a significant impact on how much it will cost to ship your products to the customer. Even if you have a retail location where customers come to buy your products, packaging will still have an impact. That is because you will incur expenses having the products shipped to your store and they will also take up a certain amount of space on your shelves.

So package you products in as lightweight packaging as you can and package them as small as you can as well. Of course, packaging should protect the contents from damage as well so you might not be able to go as small or as light as you might like.

Instant Gratification

We saved for last what might possibly be one of the strongest buying motivators there is when it comes to why people buy certain products. That last motivating factor is called "instant gratification" and it is running wild throughout society these days.

Instant gratification refers to people wanting what they want NOW rather than minutes, hours or days later. Fewer and fewer people these days are willing to wait for anything so anytime you can have a product that delivers some form of instant gratification you should jump all over it and take advantage of it.

There are a few ways where instant gratification comes into play. Here are the main few:

Be Able to Get it to Them Quickly

The faster you can get something into the hands of the customer, the better off you will be.

People do not like to wait for their purchase. They want it NOW! That is why digital products like e-books and others are so popular. People buy them now and are reading them in a minute or two! That is much better than having to wait a week for a book to be mailed to you.

So choose products that you will be able to get to the customer as quickly as possible. Products that are smaller and lighter and do not require special handling generally will be faster to ship than large bulky products that have to go by truck.

Other products, such as some chemical, must be shipped via ground services and not by air which can add several days to the delivery time when shipping far away. So evaluate not only size and weight but what the product is made out of as well.

Regardless of which products you sell, make sure you have the processes in lace to get them out the door and into the hands of the customer as quickly as possible. Often this is a determining factor when it comes to where people purchase their products. Companies like Amazon have refined this to perfection to the point where hesitancy to purchase due to shipping time frames is practically nil.

Be Able to Use it Quickly

People love to use what they purchase right away. So if any part of the product takes time to set-up or assemble, that might be viewed as a negative. Generally speaking, if a product can be taken from the box and used right away, that is a positive. If it has to be assembled, or charged, or if you have to purchase other non-included accessories, that could be a negative.

When designing a product, keep instant results in mind. When marketing products, highlight things such as no assembly required and other features that translate into instant usage and instant results.

Be Able to Get Results Quickly

A lot of products are popular and sell well because they get results quickly. Cleaning products. For example, that clean heavy dirt and grease quickly are very popular. So if your product is able to anything really fast, that is viewed as a positive.

Weight loss products that promise rapid weight loss in short periods of time are among the most popular products.

People want to lose weight but they want to lose weight NOW. They would much rather have a product that will get them results in 5 days instead of 50 days!

Sometimes we will have to choose between two products that both achieve the same results for the same cost. Whenever that happens, ask yourself which product will get those results in the shorter period of time. If everything else is equal, then I would add that product to my catalog.

Because people want what they want and they want it now. And we need to find those products that will give it to them and give it to them now.

Product Characteristics Summary

So far we have discussed the characteristics that products need to have in order to be successful. While every product is not going to have every one of these characteristics, and while not all of these characteristics may even apply to certain products, every one of them should be considered when evaluating possible products.

If you are designing or creating your own products, use this list of characteristics and try to hit as many of them as possible. This is important because the more of them that you hit, the more desirable your product will be.

It is also important to understand that all of these characteristics are not equal either.

Depending on the product involved, some might be more important than others. But some, like the need for mass appeal and overall performance and quality will apply to every product. So you are going to have to do some analysis and you are going to have to use some common sense.

But these characteristics are also important when it comes to market your products as well. After all marketing and advertising are just the ways we make the consumer aware of everything the product has to offer them. Our advertisements are giant connect the dots sheets where we take what the customer wants and point out specifically why this is the right product for them. We do not hope the customer makes these connections on their own, we lead them through them one by one.

An important thing happens when you go through these characteristics one by one. You not only get a better idea of whether or not the product is going to sell, but at the same time you get a much deeper understanding of what the product's appeal is to the customer. This allows you to market it better and more effectively.

There are going to be some of you reading this book that are going to say that going through this list and understanding these things is going to take time.

And you would be right. But ask yourself whether you would be better off spending this time evaluation things now or spending more time trying to understand why the product isn't selling and why you have thousands of dollars, or more, of inventory sitting on your shelves. Or why that product that you spent months or years creating isn't selling like you thought it would.

So far we have talked about which products were going to be good for your customers. But the fact is that products must also be good for your business as well. So now, let's talk about what products are going to be good enough for you to sell from your business point of view.

Part Three: Is it Profitable?

Choosing Products that are the
Best Products for Your Business
to Sell from A Business
Perspective

Knowing Your Target Audience

Products will sell only when you have people who will need them or be interested in them. So it makes sense to understand who your customers are and what they like or dislike. Equally important is understanding what your customers expect from you and your business. Because when you give your customers more of what they want, they will come and do business with you instead of your competition.

Learn everything you can about your customers. What do they like? What are their interests? What are their demographics? Everything we can learn about the people who are going to hopefully buy our products will enable us to better choose the perfect products to offer them. That is just another way of giving them more of what they want.

For example, if your customer base is mostly senior citizens, then you should offer products that most senior citizens use. You can offer the very best surfboards that money and buy and offer them at huge discounts but you still are not likely to sell very many. Maybe a couple as gifts to a grandchild or two but that's about it. Again, choose products that fit your customers.

Understanding your audience is also useful in understanding what type products and businesses they prefer to purchase from. If you live in an affluent area, a low-priced business model might not do very well because those are not the product they are looking for. In affluent areas you might want to stock more high-end and expensive models because those are the ones that will be in-demand.

We could go on and on about this but let's just say this:

You are going to make the most money by providing the products and services that your particular customer base is interested in. If you have what they want, they will buy it from you. If you don't have what they want, they will go somewhere else that does have it. So you need to learn, you have to listen and you have to understand as much as you can about your customers and your target audience.

This is even more important when you start your business and before you are well-known. As you become more well-known you can make your decisions based on what your existing customers ask for when they come in. But in the beginning, you are going to have to do some market research and then choose those products that your customers are more likely to want. After that the characteristics of the products will take over. But if you don't have those products in the first place, you are not going to close all that many sales either.

Competition

Like it or not, your competition is going to factor into what kinds of products you are going to carry in your store or on your website. You are going to want to carry the right products for your customer base as well as an equal to or better selection than your competition carries. Otherwise, your customers are going to shop elsewhere because they are more likely to find what they are searching for.

People go to places where they feel they will have the best chance of getting exactly what they want. They are usually even willing to pay slightly higher prices for that convenience as well. This is because convenience means saving time and saving time means saving money as well. If they can get what they want at the first stop, then the rest of their day is all theirs!

If you are operating an online business, this can be very difficult because giant sites like Amazon and other sites just carry so many products that a small business, or even a mid-sized one, would find it impossible to match. In those cases you are probably better off trying to compete in just your own niche where you will be competing against specialized retailers like yourself.

If you have a brick and mortar store then you should search the competition in your neighborhood to see what they offer their customers and then try to create your business in such a way that you can offer your customers more than anyone else. That means a better selection, better service and a better customer experience as well. All of those pieces have value to the customer.

It will probably means stocking different brands and models of products so your customers can choose the best ones for their particular needs. It is also worthwhile to have a low, mid and premium priced model so you can have the opportunity to upsell as required. Accessories often play an important role as well. Having everything your customer needs in one place can be very enticing to the customer. It is the ultimate in convenience!

The entire idea is to create a business that provides the most value to the customer. You want to become known as the first choice when it comes to what you sell. Sometimes second or third choice just won't cut it so never make that your goal. You want to keep getting better and better until you are number one. And then you need to stay there.

This starts with products and from that point on your service and your customer experience will take it from there. But stocking what your customers need is the most important. Then how you give them what you need takes over.

Shipping Costs

As far as profits are concerned, shipping expenses come right off the top when it comes to profits. So anything we can do to minimize or reduce shipping costs will lead to more profits. But perhaps the best way to minimize profits is addressing this when we choose our products or design them.

There are a few things that directly effect shipping costs. Here are some of the most common. We are making the assumption that the package in each example are going to the same place. Naturally the furthest you send something the more it is going to cost. But even those costs will be effected by each of the following:

Size and Shape

Most shipping services have standard size dimensions when it comes to what they ship at standard rates.

For example it will cost more to ship a 15 foot long piece of pipe than it would to ship the same weight product in a smaller square box. This is because it is harder to ship and load into and off of trucks.

So when choosing products, try and choose something that is smaller and compact. Even if longer pieces have to be designed to come apart and quickly be reattached, this would help keep shipping costs down. Plus, it will usually reduce damage as well since longer items tend to get more stress than compact one during shipping.

For retail stores larger and oddly shaped products take up more shelf space and allow for less product being stored in the same place. Since shelf space and warehouse space cost money, odd shaped products cost more to store and display.

Weight

Though this should be common sense, the less a product weighs the cheaper it is to ship. So when choosing products, try and find the lightest product that will still perform at a high level. An added bonus is that people usually like lighter and easier to carry versions of products. The exception being products that need added weight for stability and other reasons.

Depending on the product size and weight there also might be a need for more than one person to transport, stock and deliver these products. This would add even more cost to the product as well. Unless your profit margins are very large these expenses can quickly wipe out most profit from any sales.

Product Materials

As we already stated some items cannot be shipped standard mail or air because of the materials involved. You cannot send flammable items air freight and certain chemicals have similar restrictions. The costs for shipping hazardous or dangerous materials are higher as well. So take this into consideration when choosing products. With all the restrictions and rules to follow when shipping certain materials, it might be better to stay away from them altogether if possible.

Shipping costs are costs that really do no one any good except for the shipping companies. They make your product more expensive to purchase and that hurts your business and your sales.

The customer hates to pay high shipping costs and might start looking for sites that offer free shipping or other locations where they can physically pick up the product instead of paying for shipping. Shipping costs do not add to your bottom line and they do not add to profits either. In reality shipping costs are almost totally negative for both the business and the customer.

Cost to Produce

One of the most important considerations when choosing products is how much the product is going to cost you to either purchase or produce. These costs, in conjunction with overhead and other costs are going to determine what the selling price needs to be for you to make a fair and honest profit.

Before you choose a product to sell you need to know how much it is going to cost you when you purchase in certain quantities. Since most products cost less when you buy in larger quantity, you will have to balance cost per unit with the cost of keeping more inventory on hand.

If you are creating or manufacturing your own product, you need to know how much your costs are going to be in different quantities as well so you can forecast costs and profits. This means knowing what the materials and labor costs are per unit.

Then you can compare these costs to how much it will cost you to purchase a similar product manufactured and sold by others.

When determining costs it is always a good idea to get at least three or four quotes from various sources. We should always be looking for the best deal and the best service so we can keep profits higher while prices remain lower. Remember the more you pay for each product the less profit you make when you sell it.

This means finding multiple suppliers or vendors that stock the materials or products you need. Having this information in advance also helps when any supplier either stops doing business with you, raises their prices or stops delivering for some reason. It is never a good idea to go sole source with anything because sometimes companies can go out of business and when a supplier does that, all of a sudden you have order to be filled but no product to fill them with. But having second and third options allows you to take corrective action faster and easier than it otherwise should have.

Speaking of options, I absolutely HATE proprietary products when it comes to buying and selling them. There have been times when people have created successful businesses seemingly overnight and then have had them destroyed when the sole source for the product stops selling it to them.

If you have to buy from a single and dedicated source, ALWAYS have more than one good product so that your business cannot be held hostage by any one supplier or vendor.

Since some product designs are easier and less costly than others, make every effort to create an easy to produce product so you can pay lower costs for your products. Remember, the less you pay for a product the more profits you can make while keeping prices down. And it is always better to have control and options when it comes to where and when to buy products or materials.

Shelf Life

If a product has a limited shelf life, or if it sells only during certain and specific times of the year, this will have an impact on your entire business. With limited shelf life, you have to manage inventory a lot more closely. It is one thing to have excess inventory that might take month or so to sell off and another thing to be left with excess inventory that you will have to wait a full year before it will sell again.

Naturally year round products are the best products to stock because they are being sold constantly all year long and will provide a stable and reasonable return on your investment. Excess inventory will be sold over a few months instead of over a year or more and that makes inventory management easier and far less critical.

Another benefit of year round products is that they get a chance to build up sales momentum over time whereas seasonal items have a short attention span for customers.

This enables you to build your customer base faster and easier which is very good for the growth and stability of your business.

Another part of shelf-life is the amount of time products can stay on the shelf or in the warehouse before they "go bad". Usually this refers to foods and dairy products that have specific shelf lives. But other products such as health supplements and vitamins has a shelf live so stocks need to be kept current.

Just like with seasonal items, managing inventory for products with a limited shelf life involves more careful management of inventory as well as assurances that stock is always rotated with new deliveries going to the back of the shelve so older product is sold first before the newer product. Failure to do this will allow older product to just sit on the back of our shelves until it has to be thrown away because it has expired.

Products with long shelf lives are preferable because they can stay on the shelves longer and therefore have a greater opportunity to be sold. You can purchase a few to have for your customers and they can take as long as they want to be sold. You cannot do that with foods that expire in a week or month or two.

Give careful though to the business you are starting and the products that you are going to carry. If the majority of your products are going to be short shelf-life products then you had better come up with an accurate and effective method of managing inventory. Otherwise you will find yourself losing a lot of money because you had to throw older inventory away as it expires.

Profit Margins

Unless there are very good reasons for selling a product at a loss, there needs to be acceptable profit margins on every product that you sell. If you cannot make money on a product you should not sell it unless you need that product to fill a void for your customers.

Businesses need profits to survive and profits always come from selling products and services for more than what they cost you. So when choosing a particular product or service to sell always ask yourself "What kind of profits can I make with this product?" If the answer is that you cannot make much of any profit, it is time to move on and find something else to sell. Many a business has died a premature death because the owners failed to grasp this simple concept.

Making or earning a profit is not an obscene part of business. Though many customers think you should make just very small profits and lower your prices, the reality is that there are often so many expenses and such high overhead and other costs that high margins are not a luxury but a necessity. Your business needs profits to remain in business and those profits come from the products you sell to your customers.

The important thing to always remember is that in order for your business to be there to help your customers tomorrow, it has to generate profits today. Profits are needed to pay salaries, overhead and the other expenses all businesses have to pay in order to stay in business. If you do not generate enough profits today, you will not be there for your customers tomorrow. But try and explain that to a customer!

Profit margins should be fair and they should allow for a properly run business to make a good profit. After all those people who work for a business deserve to make a nice salary and those people who step up to open their own business deserve to get a nice return on their investment as well. But that doesn't mean that you should take advantage of your customers even if you can.

Before you can set a selling price you need to know how much your monthly expenses are going to be, what your costs are for the product including delivery and any other charges, and then what kind of profit you expect to make from each sale.

Adding those up, plus some other charges that may pertain to your business such as taxes and other fees and you have your total sales price. Of course, this assumes a certain number of sales per month which in the beginning will have to be estimated. After your business develops a history your estimates can be based on actual numbers rather than conjecture.

If you sell more than expected you will generate more profits and that is a good thing. If you sell less, you will generate fewer sales, less revenue and you will make less of a profit and if sales are low enough you might operate at a loss that month. That is why it is so important for you to be honest and base your projections in reality rather than on hopes and dreams.

Of course you also have advertising and marketing and other costs to factor in as well if you incur those costs. You should get together with your accountant to talk about expenses and revenue and profit margins. Together you should be able to come up with a fairly accurate projection and profit margin.

Profit margins are sometimes dictated by what the market will bear and what the customer is willing to pay. When you are dealing with non-essential products there is no real pressure or need to purchase so the customer can be more selective and more demanding. In those cases your ideal profit margin might not be realistic because the customer refuses to pay it. When this occurs you have to decide whether or not to continue selling a particular product or be willing to accept a lower margin.

Profit margins are sometimes lower in the early stages of the business as the business features lower prices to get people to come through their doors. In addition sometimes when a new product is introduced it may be sold at a lower price to get more sales and get the product into more hands. Often time's products are even sold below cost to get people to walk through the doors to buy them in hopes that the customer will also buy full priced items such as accessories or other products.

Just remember that your cost for the product is perhaps the highest expense related to that particular product. So choose products that are either low cost to make yourself or low cost to purchase from others. Because when the cost goes down, the profit margin goes up without having to raise the price!

Recurring Revenue Adaptability

At the heart of most successful business lies some form of recurring revenue. This type of revenue is the revenue that comes in from existing customers every month without having to advertise or bring new customers through your doors. This revenue is critical because it is revenue you get for free because no advertising or other expenses are required to bring it in.

Products that have recurring revenue capabilities can become the lifeblood of your business. Because repeat sales and accessory sales bring added revenue and increased profits into your business with little to no extra effort.

For example, look at a gas station. They sell a product that almost everyone needs and they usually purchase it many times a year. They do this year after year after year. If the average person drives for 50 years, and they purchase gasoline just once a month, that means over the course of their life they will purchase gas over 600 times. It is actually much more than that because most people purchase gas more than just once a month.

The same applies for food and clothing. People need eggs and milk and bread and they will continue to need those things every week unless they plan to eat out all the time. People also need clothing and will purchase pants and shirts and shoes and undergarments many times as well. I am sure you can see by now just how much extra profit can be generated by products that people continually need to buy on a regular basis.

Another form of recurring revenue are products that require replaceable parts that wear out over time. Items like circular saws, sanders and other tools require replacement blades and sandpaper as they get worn down or break. Usually over time the money earned through the sale of blades and accessories exceeds the profits generated from the sale of the tool itself.

And now for the greatest and most profitable example of the power of recurring revenue:

Almost everyone that owns a computer has an inkjet printer. Those printers are available very cheaply and the companies that make them often sell them for less than they cost to make! Why? Because these printers require ink and the profit on an ink cartridge is HUGE! They cost little to make and it is not unheard of for a cartridge to cost $30-60 EACH!! Imagine the profit margins on each of those cartridges!

Take a look at the type of products that you sell and see if there is the possibility of generating recurring revenue from any of them. See if you can sell accessories or service contracts on them that have to be renewed every year or so. Once people have something they usually will continue with it as long as they like it and see the value.

Very few people are going to stop using the products they bought because they need to buy ink, blades or some other refill for it. So they keep purchasing these high margin items and the businesses that sell them continue to rake in revenue from these high margin products!

If you are thinking about starting your own business but have not decided on what kind of business you are going to start, seriously consider selling products that have the ability to generate additional and recurring revenue.

This is where businesses experience huge increases in profits without having to bring new customers through their doors.

If you already have established your business, try and discover products that align with your business but have the potential to generate additional and recurring revenue. They are out there. All you need to do is search for them and market them effectively.

Recurring and add-on accessory income can generate a huge amount of additional sales and revenue for your business if you take advantage of it. All it takes is some careful planning and the right products and accessories. It is worth the time and effort to set up and your business will not only see an increase in sales it will also see improved stability from this additional revenue stream.

Examples of recurring revenue products:

gym or fitness memberships, memberships of any kind, products with replaceable parts such as blades or bits, food products, clothing, insurance policies, maintenance contracts or service contracts, any product that has a short shelf life and a continual demand.

Examples of add-on or additional revenue products: accessories, batteries, memory cards, paper and ink, cables, light bulbs, office supplies.

Is it Proprietary?

You spend months, sometimes years creating the perfect product and business only to find out that someone else has created the same product and is now underselling you and stealing away your customers. This is a really common and serious problem and you need to protect your business from having this happen to you.

Whenever you are designing your own product, it should be different than anything else out there. If it is, you need to protect that product or idea from theft by registering or patenting it. If you can patent your product or idea then no one else will be able to copy your product and sell it. The only way this can happen is if you license the product to them for a royalty or a fee.

We live in a copy-cat world where people look to see what is already selling well and then they copy it and jump into the market. If you don't own the rights to what you are selling or if the product you developed is not unique or different, people can just copy the product and set up shop in your area.

But if that product is patented and they want to jump into the market they have to go through you and pay you a fee or royalty in order to sell your product. If they fail to get permission, you can take them to court and sue them for stealing your patent. That alone will discourage people from stealing a patented idea.

You want to create a business that is also unique and patent your business as well. Maybe you do something differently than anyone before you did. If that is the case then register and protect the concept so no one else will be able to walk in, steal your ideas and create their own business.

If you feel that your business or any of your products are unique and can be patented, talk to your lawyer about this and learn the costs and fees involved in getting a patent. The process is not easy and it is not cheap, but it will protect you from the people out there that are just waiting for the next hot idea that they can steal from someone. You cannot stop this from happening but if you have a patent you will have legal standing in a court of law.

The other great thing about getting a patent or registering something unique is that often times you can license out the products for some pretty impressive fees and then let someone else do all the work and have all the headaches! If you have enough of these patentable ideas and products you don't really have to start your own business either. You can live off the licensing fees and royalties your ideas and products earn for you!

Is it Readily Available?

One very important characteristic of any product is availability. If you are going to be selling something or advertising something to your customers you need to be reasonably certain that you will be able to get access to sufficient quantity of the product to fill the demand. The last thing you want is to have people wanting to buy your product but not be able to get merchandise when you need it.

Nothing is guaranteed in life and it is always possible that a manufacturer will go out of business, discontinue a product or otherwise be unable to meet demand from time to time. There is nothing you can do to prevent that from happening. But there are a few things you can do to protect yourself from that happening.

Research the Product History

Determine whether this is a brand new product or a product that has been around a while with a solid history.

New products without a track record might cease to be in sufficient demand for the manufacturer to keep producing it or for a distributor to keep selling it. Do not trust what the distributor or manufacturer tells you as they are only interested in selling product to you and will not always be honest if they feel that will jeopardize closing a sale.

Beware of Sole Source Products

Sole source products are those products that are available from just one source. That means whenever you need to order parts or get service there is only one place that you can go. This can be very dangerous because if this one source should go out of business or refuse to sell to you, you will have no access to more product.

Whenever possible, try and sell products that you can get from more than one distributor or outlet. Not only will this help you when it comes to accessing more product in the future, it will also help you on pricing since there will be more businesses fighting for your business. Whenever something is available from only one source, you are at their mercy when it comes to price.

Research the Manufacturer

It also makes sense to research the manufacturer a bit as well. A product made by a large and well known company will be a safer bet than something made by a guy working out of his garage two blocks over.

Larger manufacturers usually do a lot of research and testing to make sure products are going to be in-demand and sell well before they produce them. So they keep producing the product for a while as long as demand remains constant. If the demand isn't there then they might discontinue the product but that should not be that big of an issue because if the product is no longer in-demand you probably won't have a lot of offers for it.

Check Out Alternate Sources or Vendors

I always recommend finding multiple vendors or source for everything you sell. This gives you leverage as far as price and service are concerned while at the same time giving you multiple sources in case one source goes out of business or no longer wants to sell to you.

You might even order material from multiple vendors if the demand is sufficient so that when one vendor might run out of stock you can just order more from the other vendor.

This will save time and make it more likely that your flow of product into your business remains steady and uninterrupted.

Identify Equivalent or Replacement Products

Sometimes even the most reliable manufacturers will go out of business or suffer damage that causes them to cease producing products. They could suffer plant damage from a storm or fire or have labor problems or any number of issues that effect their ability to get product out the doors.

Because this will adversely effect your business, you should look for similar or equivalent products that you can substitute for your current products so that your customers will continue to have options when they walk through your doors. Remember that your customers will continue to come to you as long as their needs are being met. If you don't have the products they need they will go elsewhere until they find them.

This way when access to one product stops, you can have an equivalent product, possibly another brand, to put in its place.

While it might not be the exact product, or have the same features or sell at the same price, it will give your customer an option instead of just staring at a blank spot on your shelves. Should the original product return to the market at some point you can always replace the older product with the original one and move forward.

Stockpile Inventory

If a product is really successful and you have a long track record of selling it, you might want to stockpile some inventory if you hear the product is going to be discontinued or otherwise unavailable. Sometimes manufacturers will give you notice of when they are discontinuing something and will have inventory on hand they have to sell.

This can be dangerous because you are going to have to pay out money to purchase inventory so you need to be careful that you do not buy too much and be left with a lot of unsold inventory. Also your cash flow might not be able to support that kind of expense or you might not have the warehouse / storage capability to store that much product.

All of these things should be considered before you add a product to your business catalog or shelves.

It takes time and money to research, stock and add products to your business. Your customers will come to depend on those products and expect you to have them on your shelves or on your website. So it is more than an inconvenience when a product becomes unavailable to you for whatever reason.

This is not to say that you should never sell a sole source or small manufacturers products. Instead, what we are saying is to at least factor this into your decision. Sometimes we might have two very similar products we are considering and this might be one factor that helps you decide which is the best product for your business.

The Complete Package

What we should always be looking for are products that are the "complete package" when it comes to adding a product to our business. By "complete package" I am referring to products that make sense from both the customer point of view as well as from the business point of view. These are the products that are far more likely to sell well and provide the business with decent, if not higher, profits.

At the end of this book we have given you a checklist that lists every product feature or characteristic. Use that checklist as you evaluate new or current products. Next to each item use a scale to indicate how weak or strong the product is for that item. You can use a 1-3 or -15 or even a 1-10 scale with 1 being the weakest and the highest number being the strongest.

Go through every item and then add up the total points. The more points the better the product will be for your business. This will allow you to easily compare products and help remove the emotional component and give you a more factual result.

If you want an even more accurate result, you can also add "weight" or importance to each item as well. If there is one characteristic or item that you feel is more important to your particular industry or business, add a multiplier to that item.

For example, if you add a "times 2" to "size and weight" whatever points that item will get will be doubled. You might use these multipliers to make certain that little or less important items do not skew your results. Another option might be to divide certain points by half or a third for certain less important items.

You can take this checklist and use it as you see fit and modify it so that you get the most accurate and useful data from it. You can add items or subtract items that might not apply. This is your checklist for your business and it should reflect your products and needs. It is easy to modify on a computer and you can make running changes as you see fit.

At this point we should say that this checklist is just a tool and as with any tool, it will only work for you if you use it properly. That means taking the time to enter accurate and factual data. It means being honest with yourself when you give a product a certain score. It means separating your emotions from the facts when you score items. Sometimes we become so emotionally invested in something that we rank or score it higher because we so desperately want it to succeed.

Your results are only going to be as accurate and useful as the data entered into it. You should take the time to do it right because even though you spend time on this now, it is better to spend the time now before you invest your time and money into a product than it is to spend later when you are trying to figure out why you have a warehouse full of products that aren't selling.

This checklist should be considered the final word either. Sometimes you have to go with your "gut" and take a chance on a product that you think has a great potential but might not score very high. But that is when the checklist can really come in handy.

The checklist will easily identify possible flaws at a glance. If you go down the list and see a "1" on any line, that is a weakness or potential flaw in the product.

It might be a significant flaw or it might be an almost meaningless one. But the main thig is that you are aware of it and can use it to either address the flaw or deal with it some other way.

Choosing successful products is often not a black and white process. You are going to have to do your research and you are going to have to identify and interpret certain data during your evaluation. But this tool will help you and might help sway you one way or the other if you are "on the fence" when it comes to whether or not a product is a good fit for you.

Like everything else in life and in business, this is a tool and the tool will only be as good as the person using it.

Beware of Salesmen &

Manufacturers Reps!

A lot of times business owners and people who inquire about products will find themselves dealing with either a salesman or manufacturers rep which as far as I am concerned are the same thing. The purpose of both a salesman and a manufacturer's representative are to make sales for the company that they work for.

Which means that sometimes they might not be 100% truthful or make recommendations based on your best interests. While there are some reps who will recommend things based on your situation and needs, there are more who will try to close a sale instead of finding you the best products for your business.

Just like salespeople in stores will try and sell you products that have the highest profit margins or pay the highest commissions, any manufacturer or distributor is going to try to do the same thing.

Because of this, here are a few ways that you can protect yourself from people trying to take advantage of you or mislead you:

Educate Yourself

Sales people of any type love customers who are not educated in what they want or really know what they need. Uneducated customers leave themselves wide open for all kinds of tactics designed to sell products and get the highest prices.

When a salesperson becomes aware that a customer is educated, they understand that the typical BS is not going to work and you are probably going to get a better deal or at least a more accurate and better recommendation.

Learn the product language and make a few statements about other products so the salesman will notice that you have done your homework. Then they are less likely to try to BS you with useless information and technical jargon.

Know Your Business & Your Customers

Before you talk to anyone or negotiate any kind of deal make sure you know what you want, why you want it and how much you should be paying for it. Never let anyone tell you what you need and what you should pay. You should know this going into the discussion.

Don't let the salesman tell you what products you need. Tell them what you need and have them provide the products that fill those needs. Don't let them tell you that you don't need anything or that something is not important. Believe me when I say this but 99% of the time you will know what's best for you if you are educated and informed about your customers and your business.

Do not Respond to High Pressure Sales Tactics

If a salesperson tells you that they have a special limited time offer that expires that day and you have to act now, be very careful. These are tactics used when the so-called "great deal" really isn't so great after all. They give you the short deadline because they do not want to give you time to think about the deal or to compare it to other offers or other companies.

Most commonly used in the selling of time shares, the limited time offer is used to create a sense of urgency where none really exists. This sense of urgency is meant to convince you to buy now even though you might not need the product now at all. Urgency and scarcity are two very strong motivators when it comes to buying.

Scarcity is used to get people to purchase now as well. The salesman says they only have XXX number in stock (usually just a few more than what you are considering buying) and that once they're gone that's it. You will then not be able to get them or the next delivery is going to cost more due to some price increase that is due to hit real soon.

Always Shop Around

Never take a salesman's word, or anyone's word on something at face value. There are too many people advancing their own personal agendas out there. So protect yourself by checking and double checking every offer or sales pitch.

Call other dealers. Contact other manufacturers. E-mail other distributors. Make sure what you were offered is a good deal and not something someone misrepresented to you.

This will help give you peace of mind and keep you from getting taken advantage of. Not only that but you might discover a better deal or lower prices somewhere else.

If what you were offered checks out, then call the company back and place your order. If they tell you it's too late, then I would still look for someone else to deal with. Someone else who is more reliable and reputable.

Order Smaller Quantities First

If you are dealing with a new company or a new supplier, think about ordering smaller quantities at first to try them out. Many companies will promise you the moon to get an order and then deliver a much lower kind of service and performance than what they promised.

Take some time to evaluate their products to make sure they are as advertised and perform well and are well made. Experience first-hand their delivery services and support services too. If everything is fine then go ahead and give them more business. But don't give up your current supplier until you know your new one is everything they claimed they would be.

Re-Inventing the Wheel

It might shock some people to learn that the easiest way to find a product that is going to sell is to look at which product are already selling in today's markets. When you find a product that is selling at a high rate, then add it to your catalog too as long as it is a good fit with your other products.

There are so many risks to creating a brand new product that is unlike anything you ever saw. There might be a reason you never saw it and that reason is that no one other than you and a few other people ever wanted it in the first place! Understanding this now can save you a ton of money in product development and production and finally, a LOT of unsold inventory.

Go to your competition and see what they are selling. If you see the same products in every store or website you go to that means that those products sell. It is not a fluke that you see the same products over and over in the marketplace. Businesses stock and sell the products that make them the most money. If it doesn't sell, they get rid of it!

For example if you visit 10 stores that sell products in the same markets that you do and every one of them are selling semi-pneumatic reciprocating goffiters then you can pretty much come to the conclusion that semi-pneumatic reciprocating goffiters are selling and making them money. Once you understand this you should add them to your business as well.

But if you go to those same stores and every one of them has the same product on clearance or steeply discounted, that should tell you that those products are not selling and they are just trying to get rid of them and cut their losses. Again, this is no coincidence that everyone is clearing those products out. Because of this, you should not consider bringing that product to your business at that point.

There is no shame in copying what already works unless you are stealing someone's patent or copyright. We are talking about deciding which products to carry based on what is selling elsewhere NOT copying a business model or product design.

This is especially true for new business owners or for people who have yet to develop a really good idea of what the public really wants. You can start your business with established good selling products and then, as your knowledge of your customers and markets improve, you can possibly develop your own products.

But taking note of what is selling well now will give you a very accurate reflection on the market and what products you should be selling in your business. So look at what is selling now, run each product through the checklist of characteristics and come up with the perfect products for you and your business.

Conclusion

It is a sad fact that more than 80% of businesses that are started every year go out of business within their first two years in business. Sometimes it is because the owners were not the right people for owning their own business and other times it is because they just didn't have the resources to go up against the competition. Sometimes that is difficult for the best of us.

But sometimes businesses fail because they do not have what the customers need or want and because they waste time and money choosing and stocking the right products. That is what we hope you now have a better understanding of so you can fill your business with products that sell well and reflect your customer's needs.

If you provide great service and have the products that people want, your business will succeed.

While much about success or failure lies with hard work and perseverance, making smart decisions is usually one of the most critical parts of running a successful business. After all, in the beginning money and resources are tight and you need to get the most from what you have available.

This book is not about being lazy or not making mistakes. It is about making smart decisions because you have the right information at the right time. Understanding what products have the best chances of selling BEFORE you invest time, money and inventory in them is what smart businesses do.

That is what you must do as well if you want to succeed.

This isn't difficult and it is not an exact science. You will make mistakes and you will choose a "dud" every once in a while. It happens to all of us and it will happen to you to. But if you follow the recommendations in this book and understand the reasons behind why certain products sell, you will greatly reduce those "duds" to a fraction of what they might have been.

The whole idea is having as much factual information available to you and to be able to understand that particular information. This allows us to make easier yet much more accurate decisions in less time.

Which is all you can ask for when it comes to deciding anything regarding the future of your business!

Product Characteristic Performance Checklist

Item	Points
Mass Appeal	
Long or Short-Term	
Seasonal or Year-Round?	
Solve a Problem	
Fill a Need	
Make Life Easier	
Make Someone Desirable	
Make Someone Fell Better	
Make Someone Healthier	
Save Someone Money	
Make Someone Smarter	
Easy to Purchase	
Easy to Transport or Ship	
Multi-Functional	
Unique	
Easy to Understand or Use	
Priced Right	

Attractive Packaging

Part Two: Is it Profitable?

Knowing Your Audience

Size and Weight

Cost to Produce

Shelf Life

Profit Margins

Recurring Revenue

Packaging

Is it Proprietary?

Is it Readily Available?

For More Information on
Entrepreneur Skills and Business
Building,
Please visit our Website at:

http://www.entrpreneurskillsi
nstitute.com

**For More Business Training &
Information:**

Also visit:

http://www.infowhse.com

www.ingramcontent.com/pod-product-compliance
Lightning Source LLC
Chambersburg PA
CBHW051913170526
45168CB00001B/373